The Story of How Colors Came to Be
© 2013 Lakresha Gray Diaz
Original illustrations by Lakresha Gray Diaz

From the land of fables comes the most colorful story of all. Our tale takes place on a painter's **palette** during a time so long ago only three colors exist—a time of **primary**

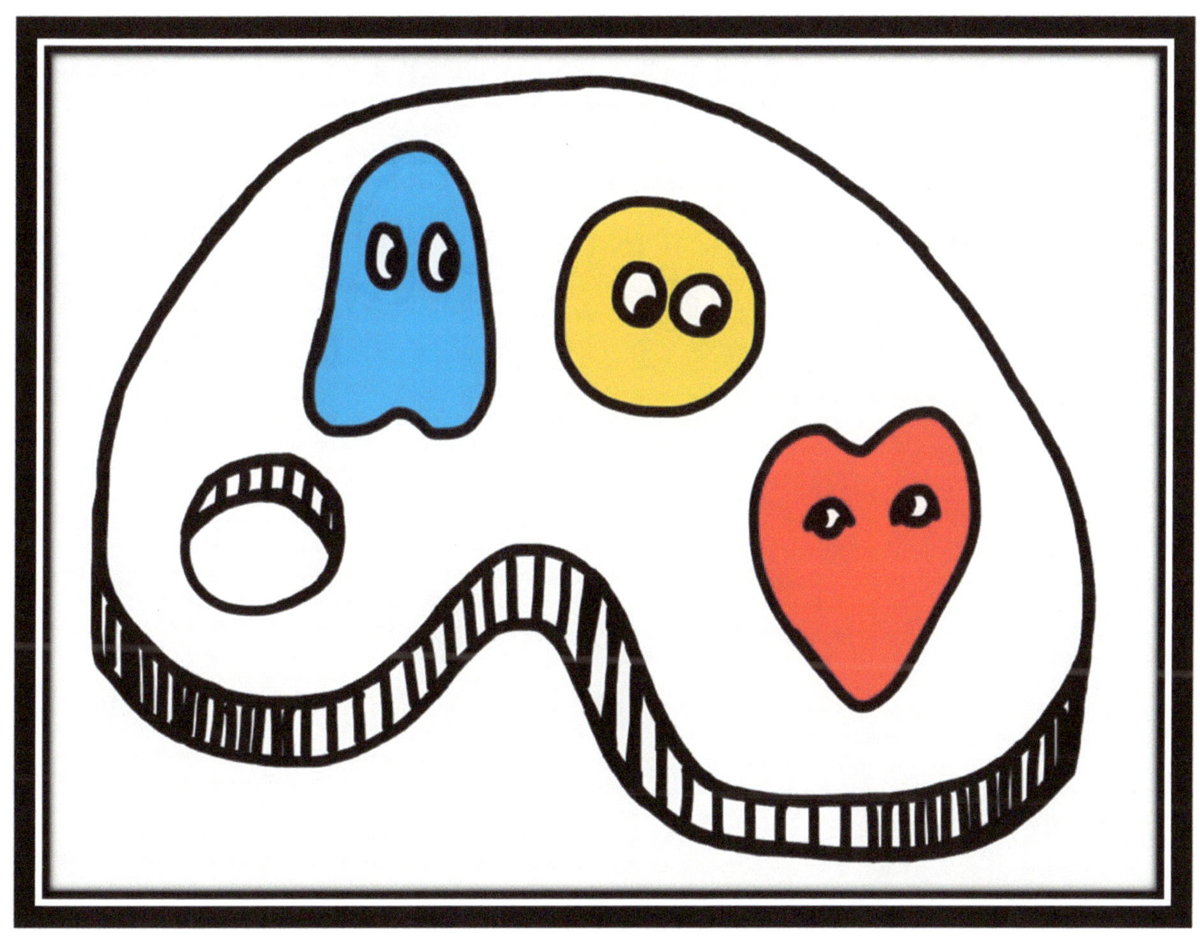

In one corner of the painter's pallet lives the proud and joyful **Yellow**. Yellow paints everything yellow and sings this song:

I'm so glad to be
Yellow, yellow!
What a wonderful color
Yellow, yellow!
Why everything should be,
Yellow, yellow!

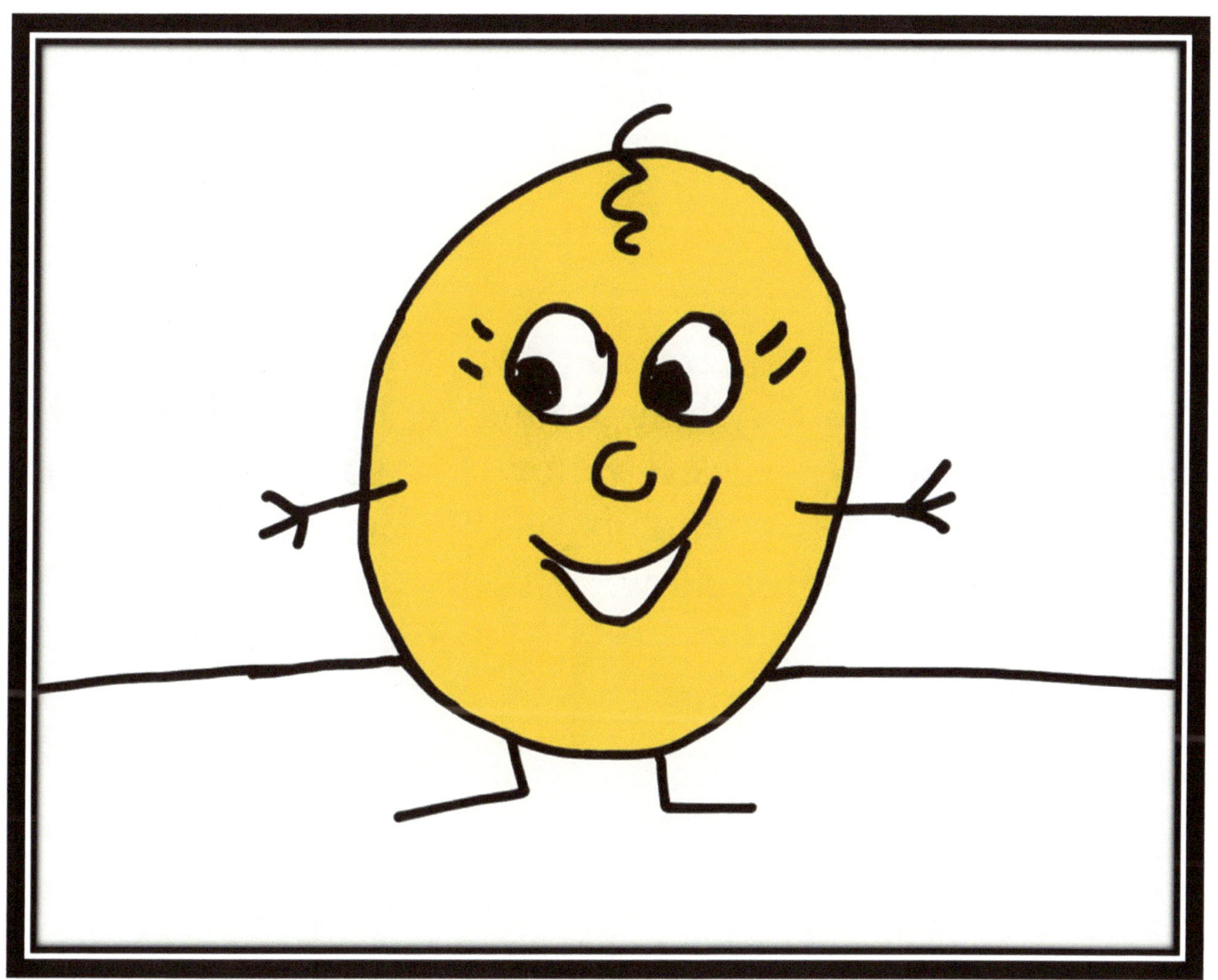

In no time at all, everything around her turns yellow. Her carpet is yellow. Her clock is yellow. Her sofa is yellow. Her side table is yellow. Her lamp is yellow. Her walls are yellow. Even her cat is yellow.

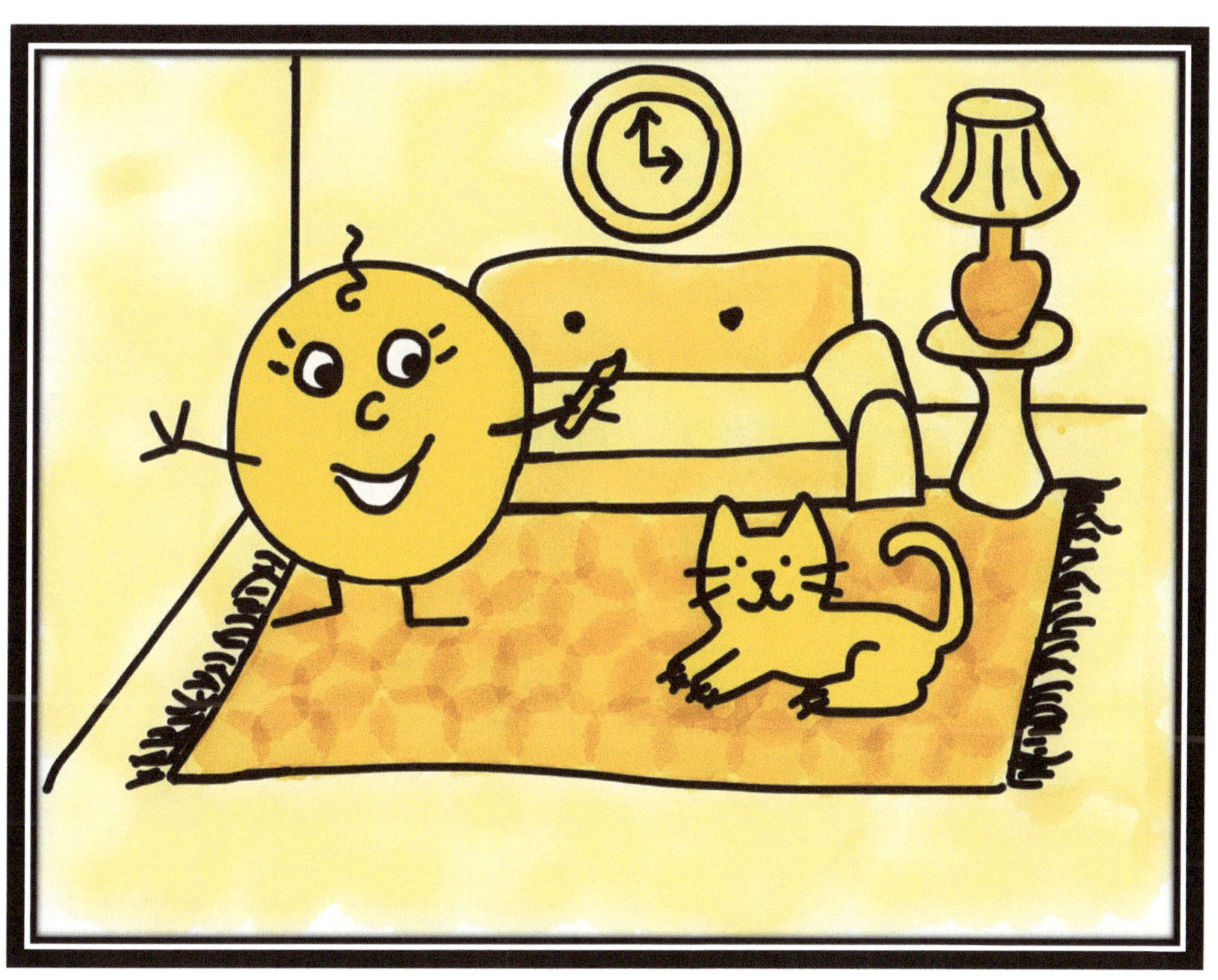

In a different corner of the painter's palette lives the delightful and clumsy **Blue**. Blue trips, spilling blue everywhere and sings this song:

B, B, B, blue,
Everything's going to be blue.
Why I think it's true,
Everything's going to be,
Why everything's going to be
B, B, B, blue.
Even you!

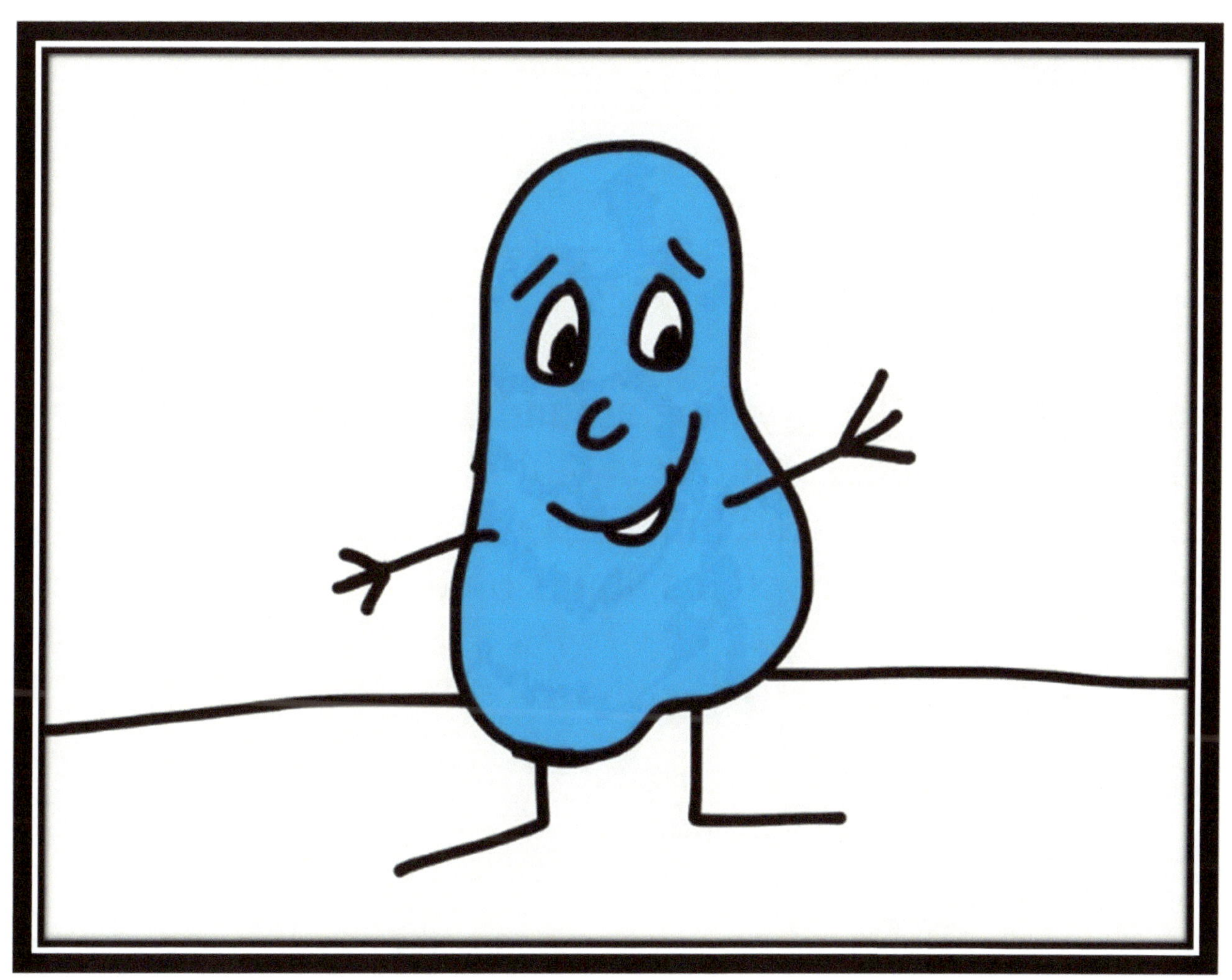

In no time at all everything around him turns blue. His refrigerator is blue. His stove is blue. His chocolate chip, peanut butter cookies are blue. His walls are blue. His cupboards are blue. Even his dog is blue.

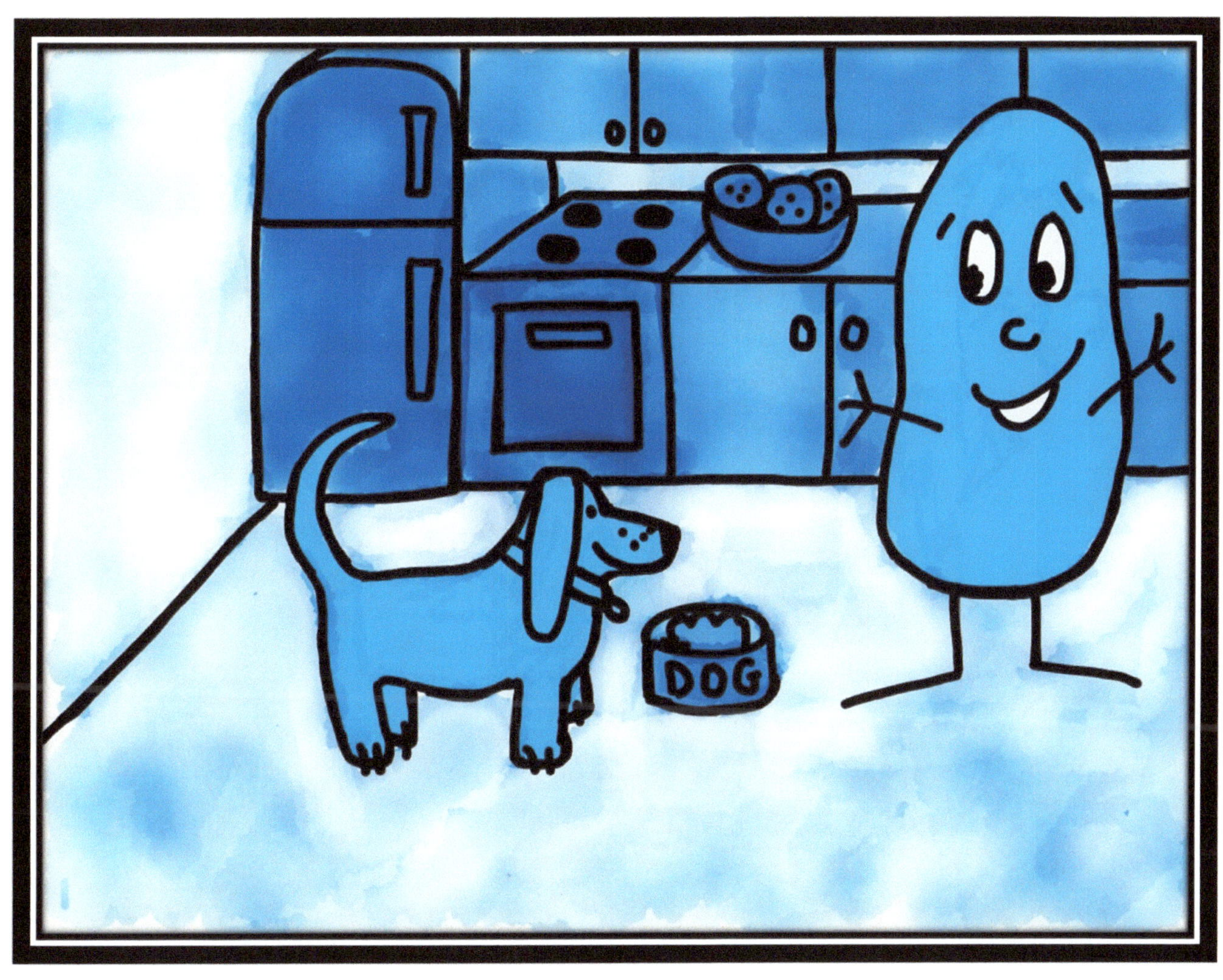

DOG

In the last corner of the painter's palette lives the fantastic and loveable **Red**. Red hugs everything and sings this song:

Oh, it's true
That Red loves you.
Yes, it's so very true
That Red,
That Red,
Loves you.

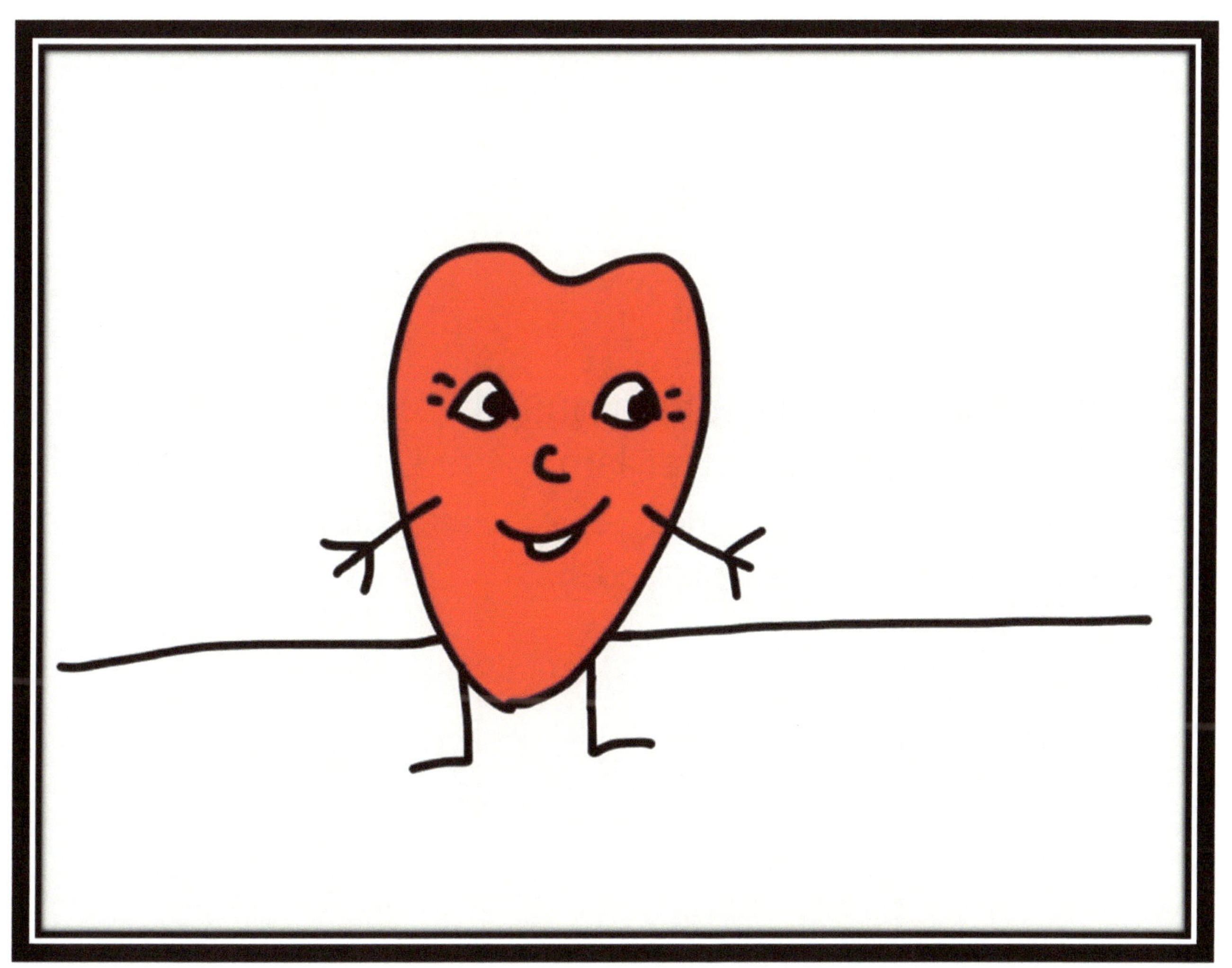

In no time at all everything around her turns red. Her bed is red. Her books are red. Her lamp is red. Her walls are red. Her pillow is red. Her painting is red. Her blanket is red. Her floor is red. Even her bird is red.

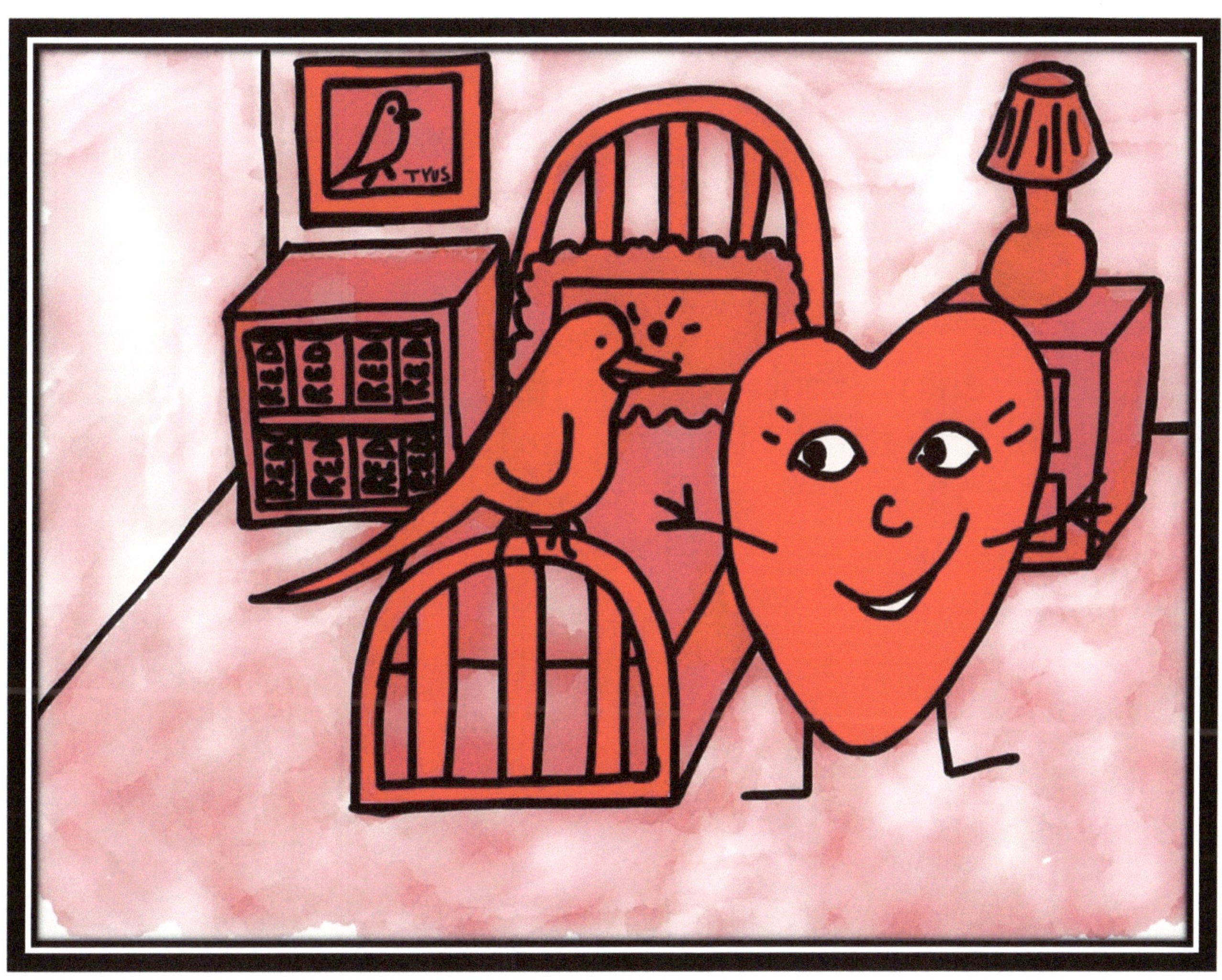

TYUS
RED RED RED
RED RED RED

Back in Yellow's part of the painter's pallet, nothing is left to paint. Big tears fall down her face, and she gazes outside her yellow house at the colorless painter's palette. She musters her courage and steps into the world without yellow. Once again, she sings and paints everything yellow.

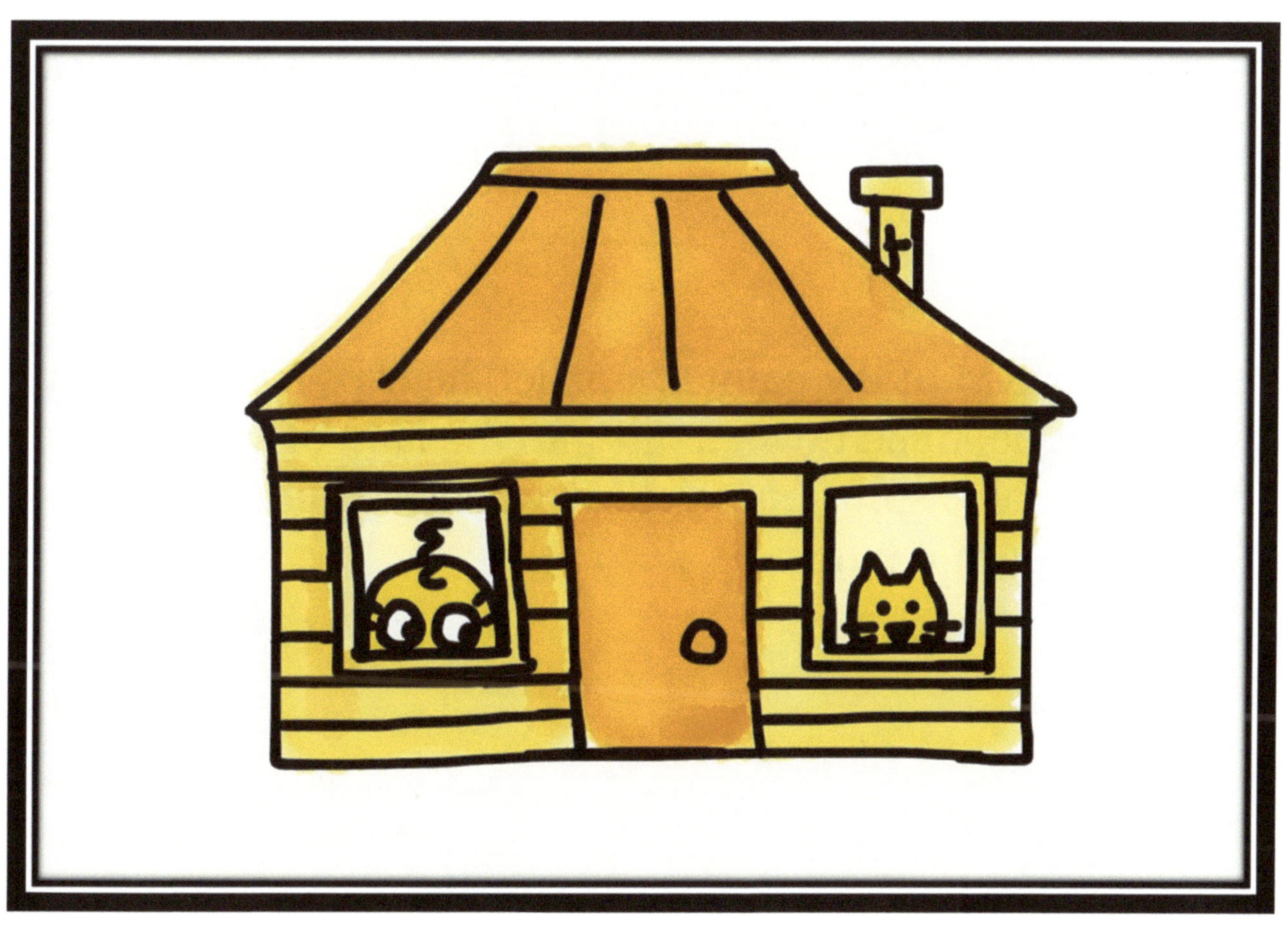

In Blue's part of the painter's pallet, he trips stumbling out of his front door and down a hill into the land of yellow. As he rolls, his blue spills out. Yellow watches Blue roll down the hill and turn it blue.

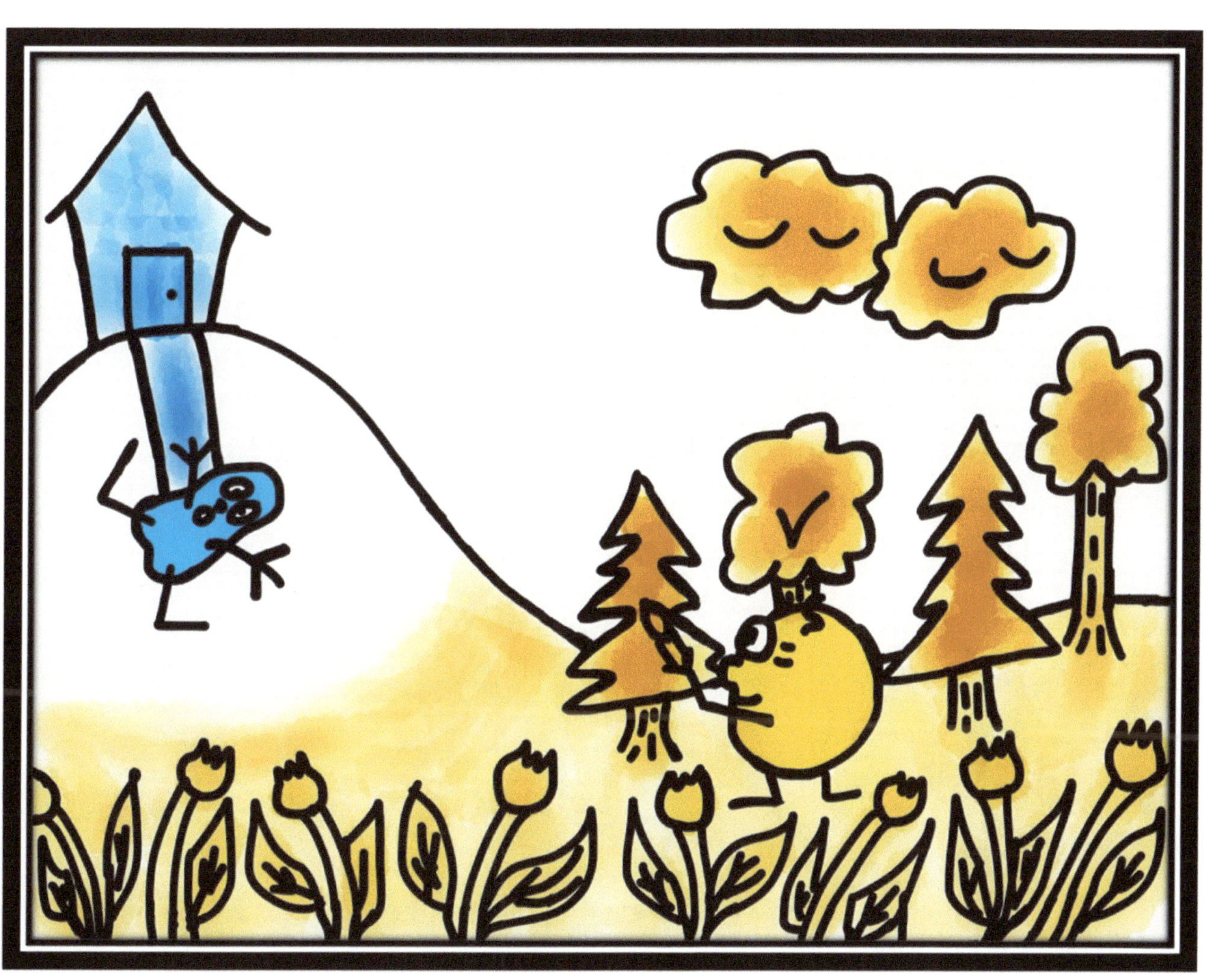

"Why, you aren't yellow," says Yellow.

"You aren't blue," says Blue.

"This cannot be. All things must be yellow!"

"No, they must be blue!"

Yellow and Blue argue and throw their colors at the nothingness until their paint mixes and forms a new color. Both Yellow and Blue tremble.

"It's not joyful yellow," says Yellow.

"It's not delightful blue," says Blue.

"This is your fault!"

"No, it's your fault!"

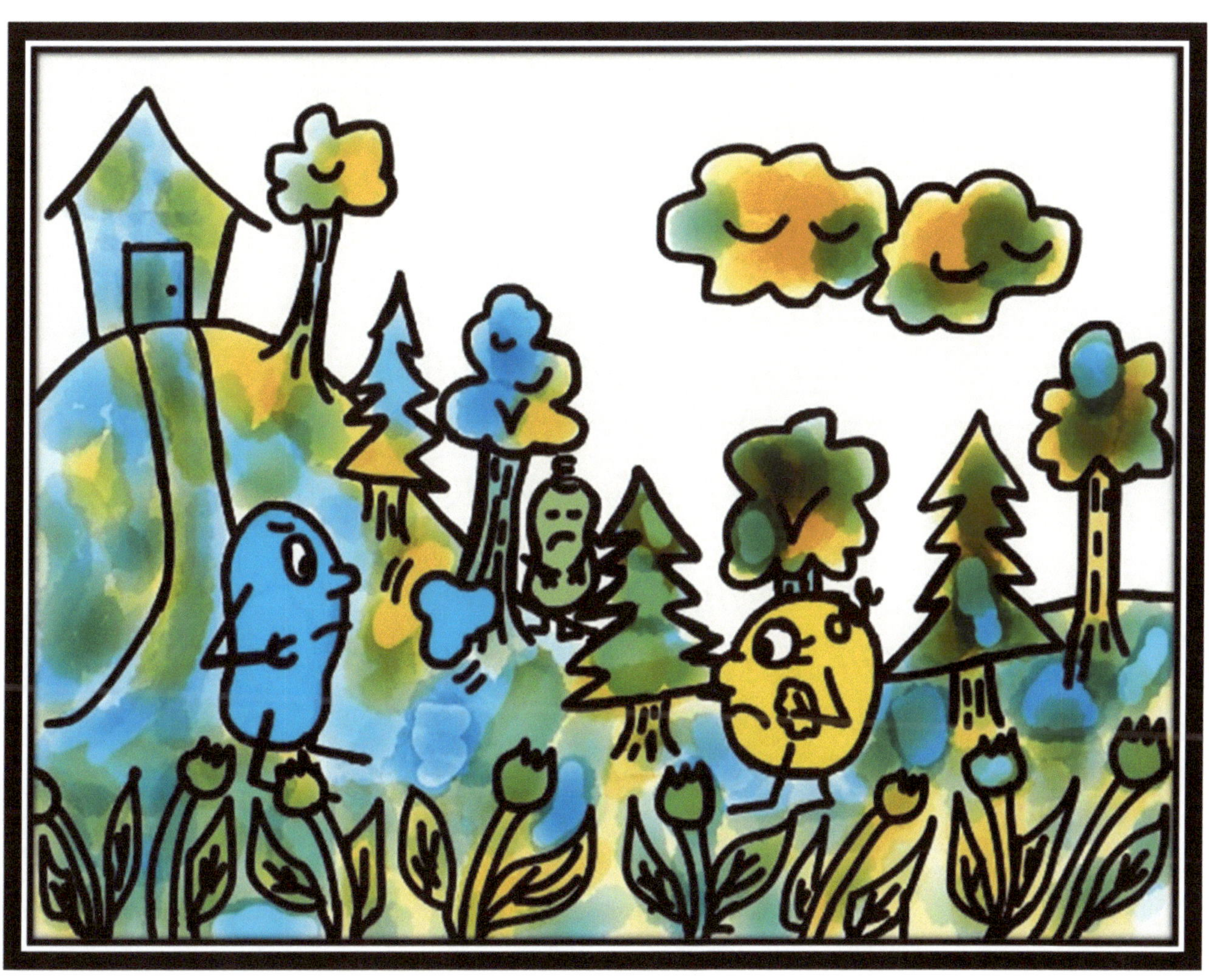

The new color, **Green**, sings this song:

Oh, I do believe it's true
You're the delightful Blue,
And Yellow is joyful too.
But, what about me?
A little bit of yellow,
A little bit of blue,
But am I joyful or delightful like you?
Oh, what's wrong with me?
I'm Green.

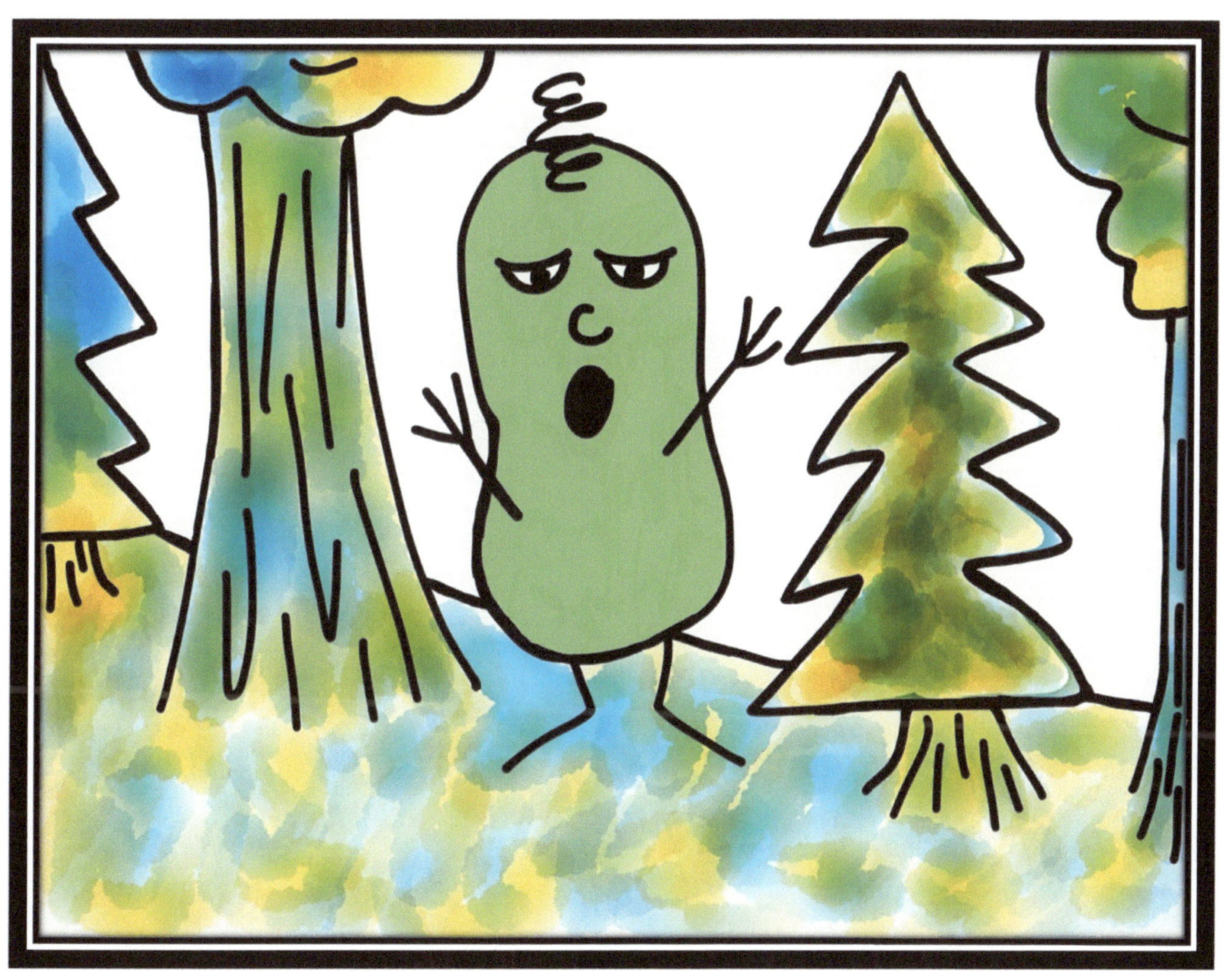

Green slumps away. Blue and Yellow examine the new world their fighting created. They agree the painter's pallet is better with Green and sing this song to him:

A little bit of yellow,
A little bit of blue,
Makes the best color ever seen,
The fabulous, delightful, and joyful Green!

Yellow, Blue, and Green travel around the painter's palette coloring things blue, yellow, and green.

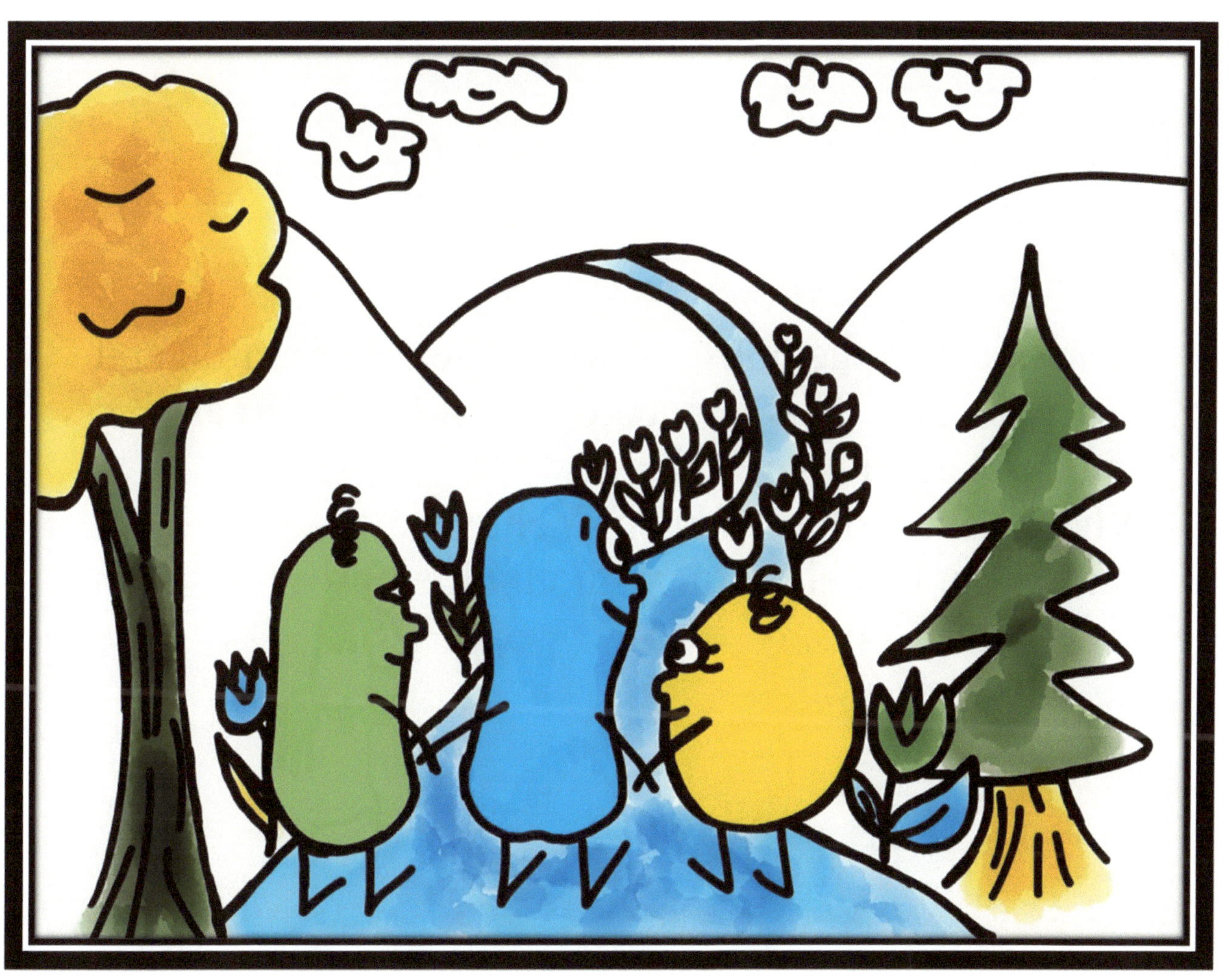

They soon find the house of Red. Their teeth rattle and their hands shake. This new color is not like them at all.

"She's not at all blue," Blue says.

"Where's the yellow in her?" Yellow says.

"She cannot be delightful without blue or joyful without yellow?" Green says.

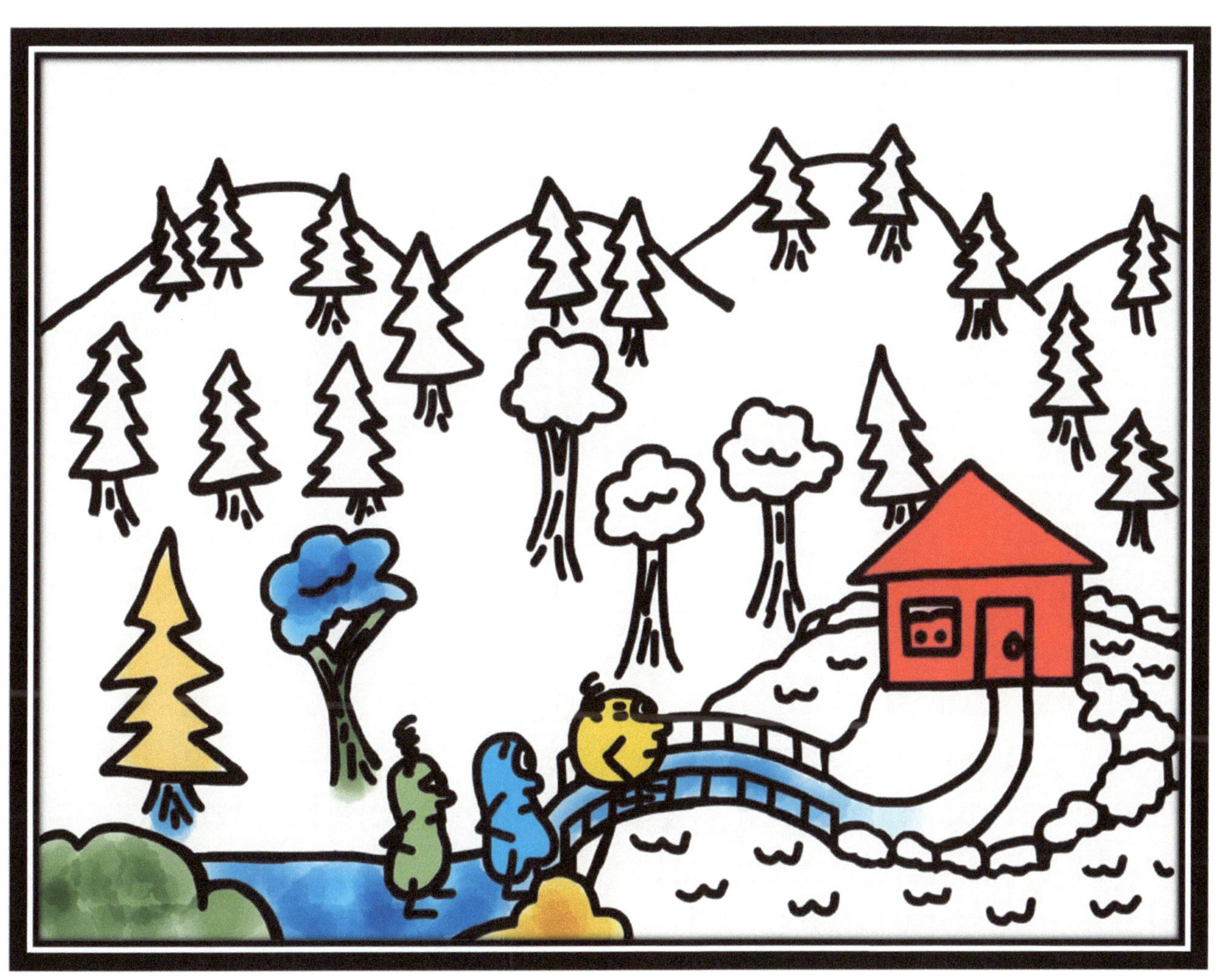

"Let's get rid of this Red!" They say together. The three colors attack anything red and sing this awful song:

We don't like Red!
We don't like Red!
We don't want her here.
A little bit of blue and yellow and green
Will make her disappear.

Red watches Yellow, Blue, and Green approach her house. She jumps around ready to hug the new colors, until she hears their horrible chanting. She quivers and hides.

Yellow, Blue and Green can't make red disappear. Blue mixes with red and creates **Purple**. Yellow mixes with the red and creates **Orange**. The new colors defend their friend, Red. They all throw their colors around and fill the painter's pallet with many different hues.

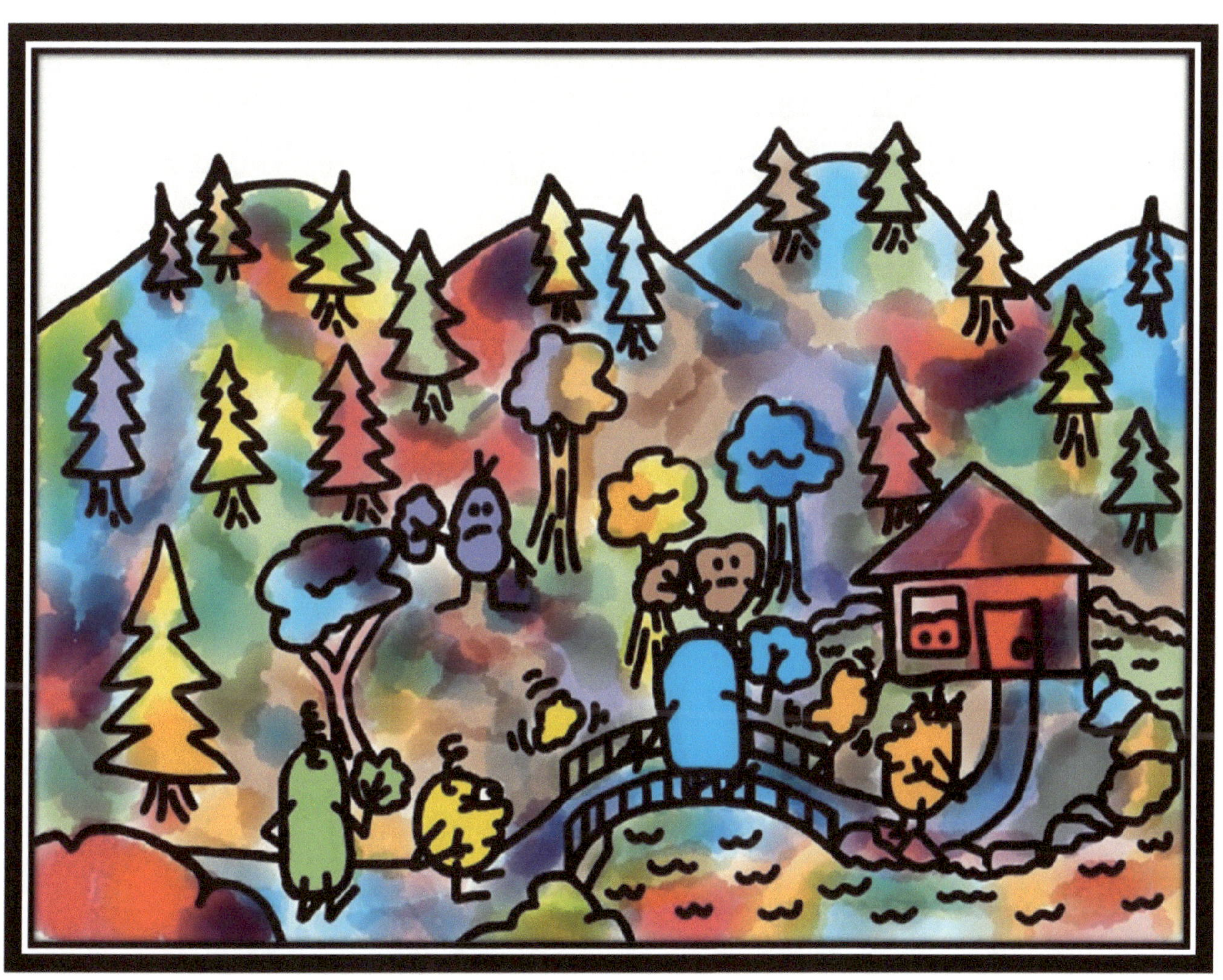

Red's need to hug is so great she can't stay in her house for long. Using love, she opens her front door. What she sees inspires this song:

Oh, what would a rainbow be
If it were just me?
Yes, we need the Primary—Blue, Yellow, and Red
*And the new colors in the **Secondary**—Purple, Orange, and Green.*
*And all the colors beyond in the **Tertiary**.*
Oh, what would a rainbow be
If it were just me?

All the colors pause at Red's lovely voice. For the first time, they notice the world created by blending their colors together, and it's beautiful!

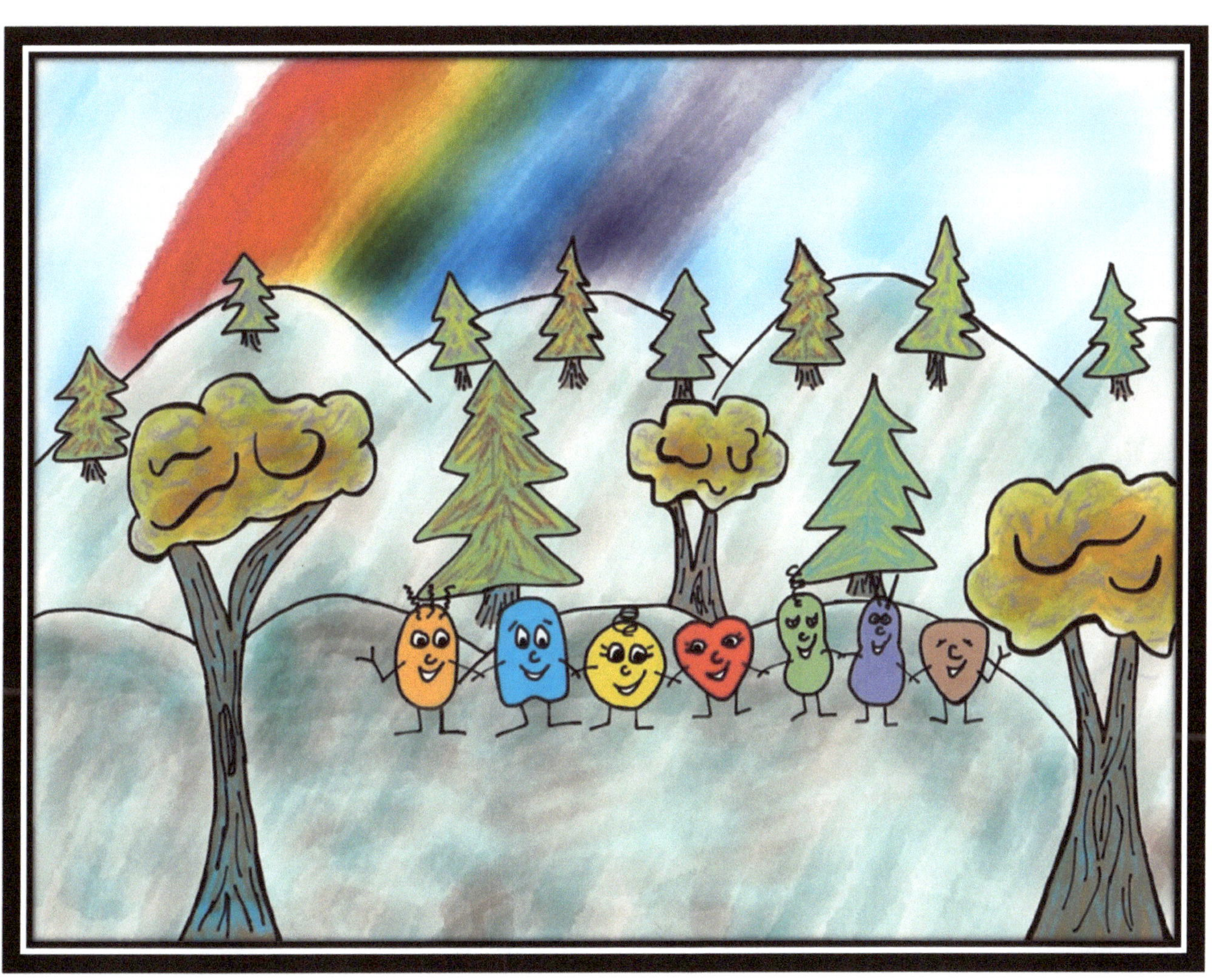

Our world with its diverse people, animals, and plants are
beautiful, too.
We just need to look.

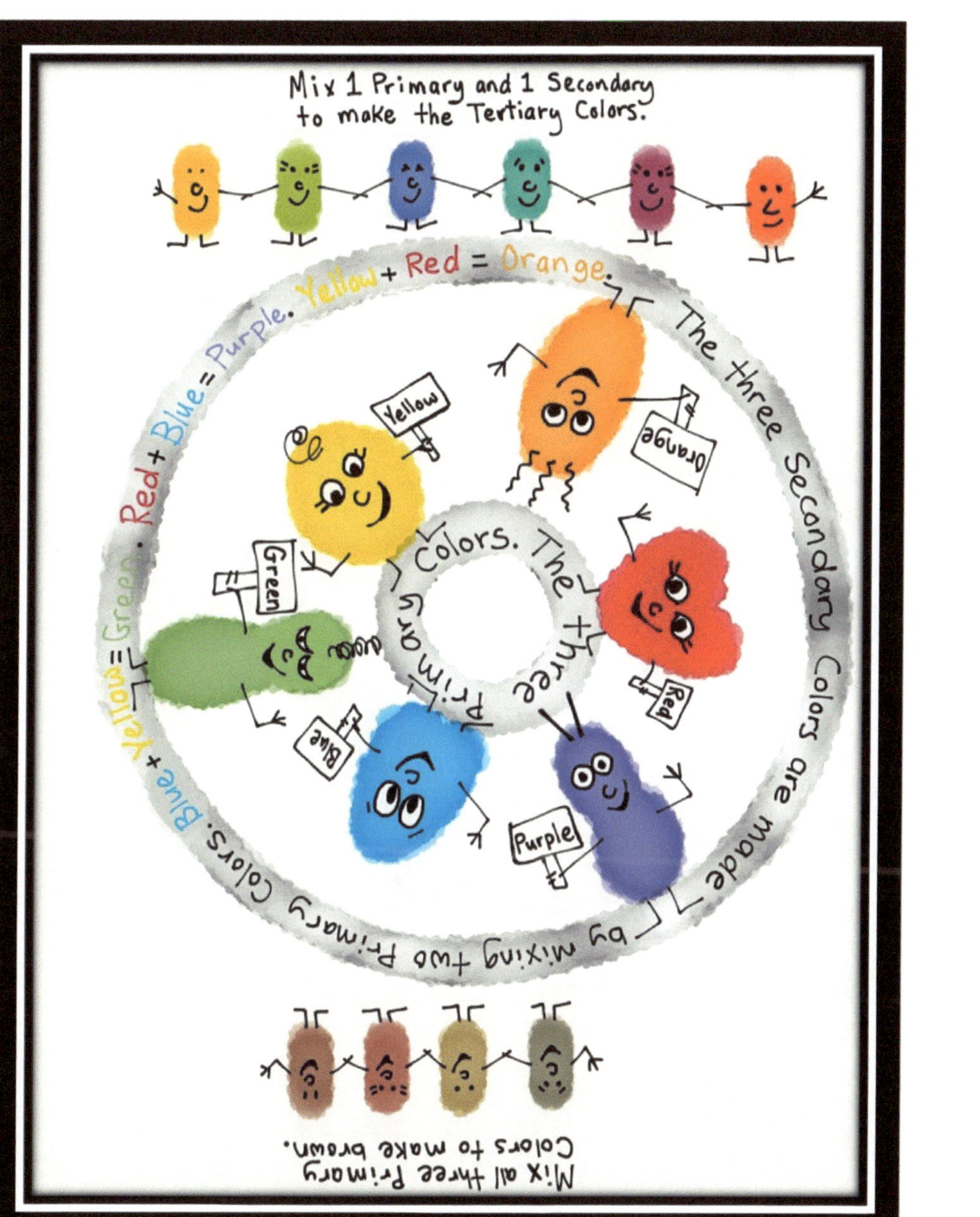

Mix 1 Primary and 1 Secondary to make the Tertiary Colors.
Red + Blue = Purple. Yellow + Red = Orange. The three Secondary Colors are made by mixing two Primary Colors. Blue + Yellow = Green.
Colors. The three Primary
Yellow
Orange
Green
Red
Blue
Purple
Mix all three Primary Colors to make brown.